Word spread that a big monster had arrived in the forest, and all the animals ran in different directions!

The little lamb, with long legs, was the fastest and ran ahead.

But the clumsy turtle could hardly move and lagged far behind.

The little monkey climbed up a tall tree to hide.
The little frog jumped under a lily pad to stay safe.

The little white chick darted into the bushes on the left.

and the little yellow duckling followed, hiding in the bushes on the right.

The bunny quickly dived into a hollow tree, while the turtle, unsure where to hide, curled up into a ball and stayed outside the tree.

"Don't be scared, little turtle! I'm new here and just want to be friends," said the ostrich as it caught up to the turtle.

When they heard there was a new friend, everyone came out, even the lamb who had run far ahead returned!